ONE HUNDRED WAYS
FOR A

*Dog to Train Its
Human*

To Heather and
the Pack

2012.

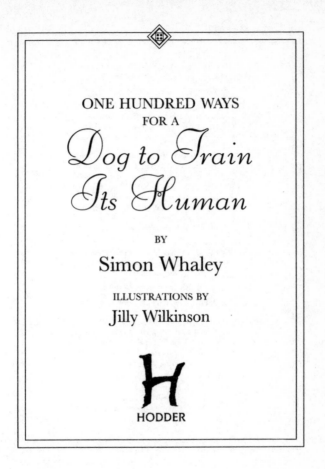

ONE HUNDRED WAYS
FOR A
Dog to Train Its Human

BY

Simon Whaley

ILLUSTRATIONS BY

Jilly Wilkinson

H
HODDER

British Library Cataloguing in Publication Data
A record for this book is available from
the British Library

ISBN 9780340862360

Printed by CPI Group (UK) Ltd, Croydon, CR0 4YY

The paper and board used in this paperback are natural
recyclable products made from wood grown in sustainable
forests. The manufacturing processes conform to the
environmental regulations of the country of origin.

Hodder & Stoughton
A Division of Hodder Headline Ltd
338 Euston Road
London NW1 3BH
www.madaboutbooks.com

This book is dedicated to Bella, who tried desperately to train the rest of the family, and me, over a period of nearly seventeen years. She always did win the `Who can keep their head under water the longest?' competitions.

Contents

Master or Servant?

Humans like to think that we are pack animals, looking for a leader. How wrong they are. Little do they realise that it is the family who are the pack, as it is they who will end up running their lives around us.

There are occasions when we can communicate with our human companions. Eyes are very important in this process. Picture the scene. It's a nice hot sunny day, perfect for lounging about in the garden. You decide to go outside and laze around, but want to take your nice clean bedding with you. As you drag it all outside across the dry dusty vegetable patch, your human may shout and stare at you. Watch those eyes. That stare will

translate as something along the lines of *'Don't even dream about bringing that lot back inside the house tonight!'* Do not worry about this. Simply glare back in a way that says, *'Who's dreaming?'* Sometimes, if that doesn't work, try a look that says, *'Sorry, do I know you?'*

Imagine that it's a cold winter's day and the back garden is covered in snow. Pure, white, virginal snow. Not a mark blots this landscape. You will have an urge to change this. So will your human. Make sure you do it first. Urinating has the benefit of changing the snow to a delicate shade of amber, and usually puts your human off from playing about in it.

The human urge to mess up a patch of virginal sand, chalk, dust or mud is not as strong as it is with snow. However, make sure you continue to be the first on the scene, just in case. Don't ignore cowpats, either.

Your human may often be told that they look like you. It's a common thought that owners look like their animals. What's often not said is which part of your body they look like. Try to ensure it's a part of your body that you can lick.

There are just some things that we are masterful at and could not possibly train our humans to do. Our tongues reach parts our humans just dream of getting to. We also have the ability to break wind and look innocent at the same time. Don't try to train them on how to do this. It'll only embarrass you.

When your human throws a stick, ask yourself three important questions:

- Is it a stick you particularly want?
- Can you be naffed to go and get it?
- Does your human look stupid enough to go and get it if you don't, only to throw it one more time in the hope that they might encourage you to get it this time?

If you answer 'No' to the first two, and 'Yes' to the third, just lie down on the ground and watch your human tire themselves out.

There is a misconception that your human will take you for a walk. This suggests that they will lead you. Wrong. The lead is affixed to you, therefore the responsibility lies with you in the direction of travel. Go where you want; your human will follow. If they try to restrain you, make some loud gagging and coughing noises when other people are around. Your human will fear that someone may report them for cruelty, and will therefore ease off the restraining. Always use this point in time to run faster.

R emember, the sooner your human wakes up, the sooner you can take them for a walk. Humans particularly enjoy getting up early at the weekends so that they can make the most of their days off work.

Always be the first to greet your human when they return home from work in the evening. Your welfare is the reason why they have gone to work. They need to earn money to buy you food and pay your vet's bills. Be the first to greet them, and don't let them in the door until they've spent at least twenty-five minutes making a fuss of you. Show them that you appreciate why they spend so long at work.

When humans return home from shopping, don't let them put the shopping away immediately.

Force them to wait while you examine the contents of all the bags first. Let's face it, you're not allowed to go shopping with them and so you ought to inspect what they've spent their money on. Keep checking all the bags on several occasions. Try to action this on a random basis. Only then can you help by unloading the contents of the bags all over the floor.

Never urinate on command. Always go when you want to go. Do not worry about insignificant events going on at the same time, such as the FA Cup final, the Wimbledon final or *Coronation Street*.

Master or servant? Just remember who shovels whose poo up. There's your answer.

Canine Compliance

Seek out any mud at all times and roll in it. Humans particularly enjoy you doing this during a hose-pipe ban.

When on holiday, always urinate when your family point a camera at you. The camera denotes that you may be near a famous landmark. Humans like you to leave a small memento of your trip on all landmarks as you pass by.

If your family point a camera at you, ignore them if they shout 'Cheeeeeeeese'. They want to take your photo. They are not signalling another food-tasting session.

When out on 'walkies' always remember to test out your camouflage abilities. Roll about in anything you can find, and then run in front of your human. Your aim is to antagonise them. When they start shouting, run into the undergrowth and hide. If they can't find you then your camouflage practice is working.

If you are busy gulping down your dinner as quickly as possible and your human shouts, '*Bolting it down like that will make you sick!*' always try to oblige.

Murphy's Law states that something will happen to you ten minutes before you all go on holiday that requires a visit to the vet. Whatever the circumstances, it will also probably require your family to fully unpack the car, too.

You won't know it, but after a good day you'll probably enjoy a dream of all the wonderful activities that you undertook. While actually asleep and dreaming, your body continues to act out those enjoyable activities, and strange noises of ecstasy emanate from your mouth. Try to dream when Aunt Flo pops round for a visit. She'll assume you're having an epileptic fit and will avoid coming round at all in the future.

The word 'vet' is an acronym derived from 'Very Embarrassing Treatment'. If ever your human mutters this word, expect the worse. Do not go anywhere near the car. Do not allow any strangers into the building. Do not hide in any places where humans have access to you.

Beware of vets with thermometers.

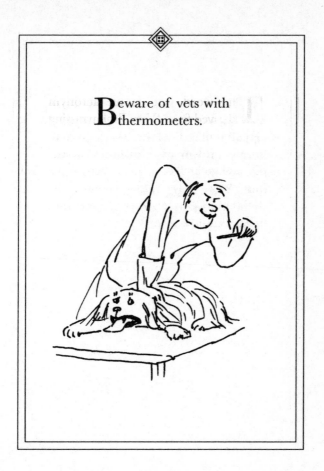

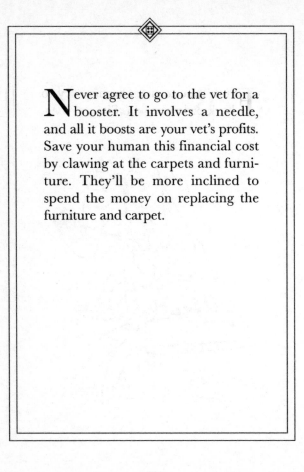

Never agree to go to the vet for a booster. It involves a needle, and all it boosts are your vet's profits. Save your human this financial cost by clawing at the carpets and furniture. They'll be more inclined to spend the money on replacing the furniture and carpet.

From time to time, humans try to bark orders at you. Sit, stay, beg, roll over, play dead – the list is endless. If you decide to join in, do it only for chocolate. Don't do it for free. Once you start, it's a slippery slope to them controlling you.

If you have something that you shouldn't have, do not let go of it at all. First, try not to get caught. You'll know the importance of the thing you've got by how long your human will chase you for it. If you're still being chased after twenty minutes, you can assume it is private and

personal and no one else in the family should see it. At this point drop it in the lap of the eldest child. They usually know which parent to take it to.

Barking Orders

Y ou may find that your human family expect you to undertake various security procedures. This can involve the phrase 'On guard!' being repeated. Upon hearing this, jump up on to the nearest chair and look out of the window. Do not worry if a human is already sitting in that chair.

Constant jumping on chairs (and humans) should force your family to consider relocating all windows down to a level commensurate with your head height. This will clearly enable you to undertake your security routine without them getting in the way.

Encourage your humans to purchase a Dyson vacuum cleaner. At the first opportunity, try to vomit on the carpet, and watch their delight as they use it to vacuum the mess. Enjoy the thrill this gives them as they watch your vomit rotating round at 3,000 revs per minute.

A holiday is a home from home. You should be able to take as much of your home with you as possible. Bedding, towels, toys, food, titbits, leads, etc., all need packing. Ideally, your belongings should be packed into the boot of the car. This will allow you to have the whole rear seat to yourself, leaving the front passenger seat for your owner's partner, three children and four suitcases.

Cleanliness is next to godliness. Never put a dirty toy in your mouth. You don't know which human has been playing with it. Insist that all your toys are washed regularly in the washing machine, and then pegged on the line to dry. Enjoy playing with your clean toy when it is dry. A good time to do this is often immediately after you have eaten your dinner.

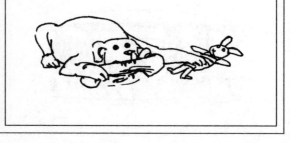

'Bark and thou shalt be obeyed' is the eleventh commandment. Remind your owner of this fact. You will know when you have achieved this successfully. You should never have to bark twice for something.

When going on holiday, always attempt to cause your driver to stop the car and pull over so that you can get out and do some 'business'. It is preferable if you can do this within ten minutes of leaving home. This has the added benefit of encouraging the children to start asking, 'Are we nearly there yet?'

If someone offers you a sweet, take it. Just the sweet, not their fingers. If it's in a wrapper, don't worry, it'll pass. If you're lucky, the kids will get the blame for taking sweet wrappers outside.

On days out to the beach, always be the first of the family to get out of the car, on to the beach and into the sea. Always be the last of the family to get out of the sea, on to the beach and into the car. Remember to shake excess sea water from your fur once you are inside the car.

When playing ball on the beach with your family, if they go and sit down, shame them into continuing to play by incessantly barking. If this fails, dig a hole in the sand next to where they are sitting, throwing the excess sand over them. This technique works particularly well if they happen to be eating.

Understand the difference between a bark and a yelp. A yelp suggests pain, such as a human standing on a tail, and is sometimes rewarded with a chocolate as an apology. Yelping when the human is in another room doesn't work. Confuse the human into thinking they've hurt you. Cowering away from them occasionally increases the peace-offering chocolate ration.

Mealtime Manners for Mongrels

Some humans will attempt to feed you just once a day. Pester them persistently for breakfast, lunch, dinner and supper. In-between snacks should also be requested at frequent intervals.

Remember, you have an ancient tradition to uphold. In medieval England, important humans had official food-tasters to check that their meals were safe to eat. You should continue this. Demand the first biscuit from every tin, the first sweet from every packet and the first

crisp from every bag. This also assists in coaching your human into providing regular snacks.

Humans may refrain from passing you food to test. To them, a piece of salmon followed by liquorice allsorts, a cake and a selection of vegetables is a foul combination. Humans believe meals should be categorised into three sections: a starter, a main course and a sweet. Disavow them of this. Food is food is food. It is this varied diet that provides you with your aromatic breath.

Drooling gallons of saliva on a trouser leg (or – even better – on tights) will encourage your human to provide you with a regular titbit.

44

Try to train your human into feeding you when you want your main meal. Ideally, you should be aiming for at least fifteen minutes earlier every day. Subtle hints such as taking your dog bowl to them or handing them the tin-opener don't always work. If you're fed at 5.00 p.m. on Monday, aim for 4.45 p.m. on Tuesday, and 4.30 p.m. on Wednesday. By Sunday you should have succeeded in being fed by 3.30 p.m. If your humans get annoyed with this, just remind them that in a further ninety days you will be back again to being fed at 5.00 p.m.

Encourage the family to take you round to visit relatives. This is the only way you'll discover those great-aunts who will lay an extra place at the table for you and serve you Sunday dinner on a plate. Always be on your best behaviour at these places to encourage even more frequent visits.

If your human encourages you to eat your dinner, particularly after a visit to the vet, treat the contents of your dog bowl with care. Look for unusual added ingredients. If at all unsure, eat what you can, then vomit it up immediately on the lounge carpet.

Sunday roasts have more ingredients than most other meals
during the week. Statistically, then,
Sundays are the best days for the
cook to drop something inadvert-
ently on the kitchen floor. Do not
leave the kitchen at all on a Sunday
morning.

If your humans ignore you while they are eating their meal, clean your genitals. It'll put them off eating, and chances are you'll be allowed to finish eating the plate contents.

Hide under meal-tables. Pay extra special attention to children. They are the most prone to dropping food. Particularly vegetables.

Any other food on the floor is fair game. It doesn't matter whether it's cat food, hamster food or budgie seed, if no one else is eating it, then it's yours. What am I saying? Of course, if someone else is eating it, kick them out of the way and get stuck in!

On no account let anyone take any food away from you. If they were stupid enough to give it to you in the first place, then they're stupid enough to get their hand bitten off.

Hounding Your Human

Never eat the brand of dog food that is on special offer at the supermarket. You'll know which brand this is; your owner will buy it in bags of three.

Water. You have a God-given right to be in it, no matter where it is or what its colour or its odour. You know you have this right, particularly when your human throws a stick or ball into the pond, lake or sea. If your human is slow at throwing an item in, ensure you enter the water first to signal that you wish to play this game.

Always make sure that you have more energy at the end of a walk than you did at the beginning. Believe me, humans love the futility of taking you for a walk to tire you out.

Humans believe that you have exceptional hearing. You have the ability to hear high-pitched whistles that they can't. Train them, though, into realising that you have 'different' hearing. Ignore them completely when they are standing next to you and shout 'STAY!' yet always go running when you hear them opening a packet of biscuits two miles away.

Sunday dinners are the best. They take the longest to prepare. Assist this process by lying in the most awkward place on the kitchen floor.

Encourage your humans to prefer self-catering holidays. They'll be more likely to take you with them, instead of putting you in a kennel.

Never let them book holiday accommodation with a spiral staircase. It'll send you round the bend. And eventually them, too.

Insist on holiday accommodation that has decent television reception. You should still be able to watch *One Man and His Dog* on BBC2 without any interference. Even better if your human finds accommodation with satellite or cable television. This will enable you to watch the repeats on UK Gold.

The best holidays are those where you stay within rolling distance of the sea, mudflats, nearby sewage system, slurry pool or man-ure mound.

If your human encourages you to fetch the paper, ensuring that you put your teeth through the sports pages and the celebrity gossip pages should put paid to future requests.

Christmas is about giving. Give your humans some fun by unwrapping all the presents under the Christmas tree. That way they'll have fun working out what the present is, who bought it, and who they bought it for. Remember to eat any sweets that you come across.

Try to learn as many TV theme tunes as possible and then sing along with them. Stupid humans may throw items at you to shut you up. Intelligent humans should get out a video recorder and film you howling, which they will then send to their local television company in the hope of winning £250.

If all your family are sitting in chairs and on the sofa, half-asleep watching television, one good way to wake them up is to sit up and start scratching your back with a hind leg. Occasionally switch legs and scratch another area of your back. Eventually, the whole family will feel the urge to scratch themselves. That's the time to leave the room.

Personal Pooch Pampering

Hot Bedding. Demand this right. Don't worry, humans are used to a similar principle where they work, called Hot Desking. It means that they don't always sit at the same desk every day to work. Demand Hot Bedding rights. Never sleep on the same human bed twice in a row.

Hairdressing skills should be encouraged. How else will they get that dung-infested clump from under your armpit without you having several bald patches?

Never let your human blow-dry you with a hairdryer. Believe me, tomorrow you'll wake up and your fur will be so fine and wispy you won't be able to do a thing with it.

When packing for a holiday begins, ensure plenty of towels are packed for you. A wet, sandy dog creates many wet, sandy towels very quickly indeed. Each day of the holiday should be savoured for the opportunities it provides. Each new day should not begin with you carrying around the remnants of yesterday's adventures.

Make the very most of Sunday dinners. They usually contain a bone. If you are successful with the soulful eye look, you should succeed in being given the bone. Savour it at your pleasure, but if your humans give you the bone while they sit down to eat their meal, always maintain one eye on the floor beneath the table. Dash to anything that plummets towards this floor. Your bone will still be there when you return.

Always offer to wash up after a Sunday roast. A tongue cleans plates, cutlery and roasting tins far better than any leading brand of washing-up liquid.

Old age will make you more susceptible to draughts and stiff joints. Demand better home comforts. An old mattress is better than those dog beds from the High Street store. A 15-tog duvet provides more warmth than a thick blanket. Relocate all this to the nearest radiator.

If you acquire these comforts in your old age, don't be afraid if your human becomes concerned as to whether you want any company during the night. Some may even sleep on the floor to be nearer to you. Do not feel guilty about this now that you are on a mattress and nestled in a duvet. Share with them that old flea-ridden beanbag that you've spent the past fifteen years sleeping on.

Learn to bite your nails. It sounds disgusting, tastes great and leaves a good mess on the carpet. It also prevents your human from purchasing nail clippers and trimming them for you. If they do buy such equipment, never let them use it. It may start as wanting to clip a nail, but without proper training you could lose a leg.

Enjoy being stroked. Foster stroking as a means of helping your humans to relax. A good time to relax is just after eating Sunday lunch. Help them stroke you by being close to them. Preferably on their lap.

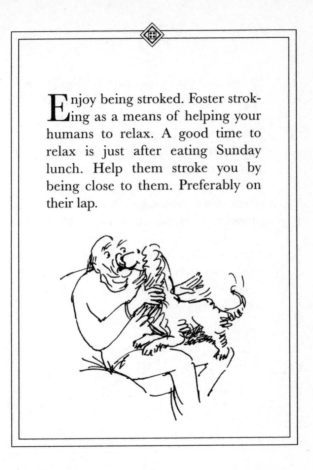

Encourage non-dog-owners to stroke you. When out on a walk with your human, go up to other people, introduce yourself and encourage them to make a fuss. This also helps in extending the time out on a walk. Remember, though, that if you approach a human of the opposite sex to your owner, it can backfire. That human may ignore you in favour of your owner. If this happens then it becomes appropriate to start breaking wind rather loudly.

If the noise of human mating wakes you up, locate where the action is taking place and try mating with one of the legs of the humans. Continue until the human complains of cramp. This should eliminate any romance between the humans and remind them they are acting more like animals.

If human mating continues, make loud retching noises and act as though you are about to vomit in the female human's handbag.

Mongrel Moultings

There will be times when you suffer in your role as master of the house. Take the 'fetch a stick from the water' game. No matter how hard you try, it is nearly always

impossible not to get water in your ears. This can play havoc with your hearing, particularly of food items. Ensure that you clear excess water by shaking your head vigorously. This also benefits in shifting earwax. A successful ear-canal cleansing can often be seen on nearby wallpaper and items of furniture.

The washing of bedding is a two-way process. Continuing the Hot Bedding principle, when your human family washes all the bedding, you must find the time to test this bedding out once clean beds have been made. Most washing powders and fabric softeners claim to bring the outdoor freshness indoors. You're the outdoor expert. You're the one with the sensitive nose. Only you can check out this claim. It's tough, but try to spend at least three hours asleep on each bed immediately after it has been made, to check for 'freshability'. Repeat this test frequently.

Humans like clothes. Particularly women, although some men have an unhealthy attitude to wearing very expensive clothes too. Encourage them to save money by not buying new clothes. Always rub your fur coat against any human clothes, especially if they happen to be wearing them at the time. When they have clothes covered in your own fur, they will soon realise that these are the clothes they want to wear, and will refrain from buying anything new or in a colour that contrasts with your own fur.

A tip to quicken the pace of adding your own fur to your human's clothing is to constantly wriggle about on your back in the living room. This gives your fur its own static electricity and enables each hair to fly around the room looking for a garment to attach itself to. This is best operated by rolling on

the floor energetically, then standing up and shaking vigorously. You can now leave the room and allow the flying hairs to get on with their job while you go and do something more useful elsewhere.

Remember, no matter how much you moult, you will never go bald. And that really annoys humans. Particularly the bald ones.

If another dog offers you fleas, always accept. It's rude not to share. Remember to share them with everyone at home.

Obedience classes are for wimps. If you find yourself being tricked into attending, do whatever you can to embarrass your owner. Stoop as low as necessary to ensure that your human never wants to go through that again!

A visit to the vet can result in the need to take pills. When your human pushes these into your mouth, hide them under your tongue. Wait ten minutes then demand to be let out into the garden to do some 'business'. Spit the pills out into the flowerbed.

If the pills are of a chalky substance, roll them around your mouth until they have almost disintegrated, then spit them out on to the carpet. Hopefully they will congeal with the carpet fibres so they can't be picked up.

Always shake excess moulting fur off when a human has just hoovered. It allows you to monitor how much hair you are losing.

Never let a human groom you with a brush they wouldn't use on themselves. Brushes with serrated-edge pins are the worst and should be avoided at all costs. Encourage your human to demonstrate the brush first, on their mohair jumper.

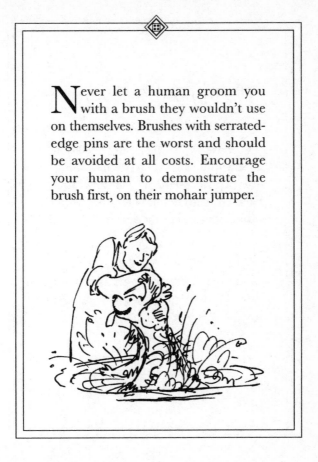

Puppy Problems

Always watch the family television, and learn. Pay particular attention to advertisements with toilet rolls. Follow the guidelines carefully in this canine service broadcast.

Part of growing up involves understanding that your human family will always come and get you. When you swim to an island in the middle of a pond, never swim back. This trains your human owners into retrieving you, demonstrating their love for the water and you at the same time. This also works with mudflats and quicksand.

When playing in water, always retrieve the item your owner has thrown and drop it at their feet. As they bend down to pick it up again, remember to shake your coat vigorously to expel surplus water in case they throw the item back in the water again.

Sunbathing is good for you. Some experts believe that the sun can give your body extra vitamins, particularly as you grow. Always lie outside in the sunshine if you can. Stop your human from making too much noise in the garden on a sunny day by lying in front of the lawn mower.

Remember that cowpat you rolled in? Always keep it hidden from your human for as long as possible. When you've been lying in the sun it will become dry and hard. Your human owner will then cover you in water from head to tail to wash it off. Insist on being allowed outside again in the sun to dry off.

'Walkies!' is a phrase that you will come to enjoy. It's an opportunity to enjoy some exercise. However, 'walkies' isn't always suggested when it's convenient to you. Never agree to 'walkies' at half-time during a football match on the television. Wait until at least the penalty shoot-outs.

'Walkies' should be regular. Humans like regularity. Annually is a particular regularity that humans like. You need to aim for three times daily as a more suitable regularity.

If your human is new to being trained by a dog, you need to make extra special efforts to remind them that you will be there to coach them. Always leave a toy on the top stair for them to trip over. Hide that Brussels sprout you've been chewing since Christmas in one of their slippers. Throw your dung-infested tennis ball into the bath while they're having a wash.

Play is an important development tool for a puppy. Demand to play when it goes quiet in the household. About three o'clock in the morning is usually quiet.

There's a knack to taking a drink of water from your water bowl. Curl your tongue backwards to scoop up the water and throw it to the back of your throat. Swallow what you need and then allow the rest to roll back into your cheek and jowls. Repeating this, especially on a hot day, enables you to evenly distribute this excess water from your jowls to any floor you happen to be walking across. Humans enjoy mopping this up afterwards.

You may often be compared to the youngest child in the house. If so, try to act like one. Whenever your human buys you a new toy, remember to play more with the packaging.

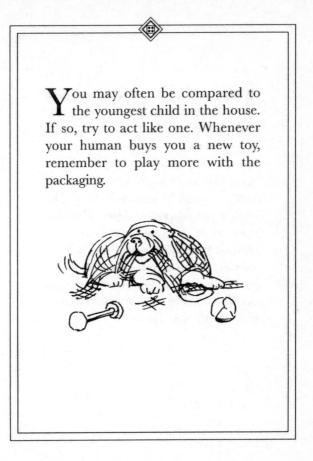

Part of the joy of joining a new family is exploring the new home and its garden. Your first few days in the home should be spent tasting everything. Banisters, carpets, furniture, plastic storage containers and even human beings, all should be given a sniff, lick and a bite. Humans may try to persuade you not to do this. Get round this by doing it while they're not looking. Remember to look innocent if the chair leg you've been chewing collapses when a human sits down on it.

D on't forget to explore the garden. Spring is the best time for this. Everything is new, fresh and colourful. Daffodil heads are bite-size. They look particularly good spat out, too.

Humans often use the phrase, 'Bringing the outdoors indoors'. Try to build on this. Remember to bring in all your discoveries to show your human companions. Dead birds, live mice, frogs with no legs and slugs will all make your humans quickly take them back outside again. This new game can last for hours if you manage to bring the same animal back inside again quickly.

And Finally ...

Remember, a family is for life, not just for Christmas. But loyalty only lasts as long as the biscuit tin is open.